War Poems

Also by the author:

Hummingbird (Vantage Press, 2004)

War Poems

Pearlina Kline

VANTAGE PRESS
New York

Cover design by Susan Thomas

FIRST EDITION

Copyright © 2007 by Pearlina Kline

Published by Vantage Press, Inc.
419 Park Ave. South, New York, NY 10016

Manufactured in the United States of America
ISBN: 978-0-533-14887-5

Library of Congress Catalog Card No.: 2004091581

0 9 8 7 6 5 4 3 2 1

To the world

I dedicate this book

Contents

Lost Angels   1
How Would You Feel?   2
Rescue Me   3
Hail to the Troops   4
Sorry   5
Sandstorm   6
Media   7
Kids   8
The Troops   9
Mistakes   10
Sacrifice   11
Explosions   12
Saddam   13
You and Me   14
My Daddy   15
Mommy   16
Why?   17
Son   18
Baby   20
Daughter   21
Combatant   22
Our Dead   23
The British   24
Fear   25
Our Mighty Military   26
Hero   27

The Reporters Who Died   28
Effects   29
Wind   30
Sleep   31
The Coalition   32
The Cost of Freedom   33
Taskforce Ironhorse   34
My Poems   35
The People   36
Still Dying   37
Is It Over?   38

War Poems

Lost Angels

Lost angels here and there
Lost angels everywhere
They go to defend
Lose their lives in the end
For our lost angels
We must win

Our angels are lost
What can we do
They can't fight alone
We must fight too
We'll fight for their life
They are worth another strife

We promise them now
To never relinquish that vow
To demolish that wretch
That caused us this fret
They will always be on our mind
We won't leave anyone behind

How Would You Feel?

How would you feel if you were there?
Trying to avoid the missiles and hardware.

How would you feel if you were there?
You would always have to be aware.

Of the danger around, yes everywhere.
What is it like to feel so much despair?

How would you feel if you were there?
Worrying about how humanity will fare?

How would you feel if you were there?
If you are still here and service, beware.

Of the task and sorrow that awaits you there.
Where other strong men and women are already aware.

And trying to amend the problems that Saddam
And his regiment put there.

Rescue Me

Rescue me
Please rescue me
Cover me
Protect us please
We are trying to escape
The war and the raid
On our homes and lives
I am really afraid
My child is very young
Her life has just begun
She is really, really scared
Of the noise and warfare
This is my husband
And this is my brother
We can't make it much farther
We don't have any water
We are in a bad state
Please help us reclaim our fate
Our country is where we should be
We don't want to leave
We just want to be free

Hail to the Troops

Hail to the troops
They come to avail
Hail to the troops
We will have no more wail
Hail to the troops
The ones that sail
Hail to the troops
All those on the trail

Hail to the troops
We thank them for coming
Hail to the troops
We are glad they are not sullen
Hail to the troops
They are our friends we see
Hail to the troops
We are going to be free

Sorry

Sorry that we had to come
We know that you don't want us here
We really wish you wouldn't fear
Our friendly troops, their lives are dear
To their families that fear, like you fear
For your families, religion, and country you adhere

Their families pray just like you
That one day the world will find a way
To live and get along each and every day
Our troops are trying to find the key
They know that all mankind should be free
So they are working very hard that you can be

Just give them a hand
Please don't try to defend
A ruler that only intends
To keep you from amends
He wants you all to be
His slaves instead of free

Sandstorm

Sand on the ground
Sand all around
Sand in the air
Sand in my hair

Sand under my feet
Sand in my seat
Sand on what I eat
Sand in my teeth

Sand is on the line
Sand we tread all the time
Sand tries to blind
Sand in our face and on our mind

Sandstorm, sandstorm
Go away
Sandstorm, sandstorm
Please don't stay

Media

The media is here to stay
The media is here at bay
They want to see what happens today
They want to know what does anyone say

It is a dangerous way to get a story
Oh those reporters they make us worry
We only hope that they won't be sorry

They put their lives in so much danger
I'm sure they feel just like a ranger

It's hard to understand what drives them so
For most of us we will never know

They will get their stories
You watch and see
They want to know if the people will be free

Kids

The kids are frightened
Yes they are
The kids are frightened
Of the war
The kids are frightened
To see their land destroyed
The kids are frightened
Something we couldn't avoid
The kids are frightened
All they do is cry
The kids are frightened
They don't need to die
The kids are frightened
Please keep them safe
The kids are frightened
Of what is in their face
The kids are frightened
Let's give them a smile
The kids are frightened
They will come around in a while
When they see that we are their friends
And feel they are free
They won't be frightened anymore
And kids they will be

The Troops

We are proud of you
You are the ones we look up to
You're the very best
At any quest
You make us proud
We are shouting aloud

We are proud of you
And all that you do
To protect all men
And all of our lands
You make us happy
We clap our hands

We are proud of you
We love you dear
You keep us safe
With you here we do not fear
You keep us free
We are praying for thee

Mistakes

Mistakes will happen
Hopefully only a few
Mistakes will happen
We are human just like you

We regret any error
And hope none were hurt
We regret any error
We are not trying to ruin your worth

Mistakes will happen
We are sorry for the few
Mistakes will happen
We lost a few from them too

Sacrifice

Don't sacrifice your life for him
Don't sacrifice your life it's a sin
Don't sacrifice your soul to the wind
Don't sacrifice your kids and your kin
Don't sacrifice your life you won't win

What he told you would happen
Is a lie
Your body, your soul, your spirit
Will die

If you sacrifice your life
You will be doomed
Is not your life worth
More than gloom?

You won't go to paradise
If you take your own life
You belong to the Deity
He decides your destiny

When he is ready for you
He will come to meet you
If you take that away from him
You will never live again

Explosions

Explosions are heard everywhere
Explosions are seen up in the air

Explosions are lighting up the night
Explosions are causing oh such fright

How many explosives will you need?
How many explosions to get us to heed?

The explosives are destroying our land
The explosions that are done by your hand

Stop your explosions we've had enough
Stop your explosions they are causing a rut

Explosives are not the key to peace
Explosives cause us so much grief

Please try something else
The explosions are too hard

If you can't find the answer
Please ask the Lord

Saddam

Saddam, Saddam
Where are you at?
Saddam, Saddam
You're like a cat
Saddam, Saddam
We are here to seek you
Saddam, Saddam
Don't play peek-a-boo
Saddam, Saddam
We are so ashamed
Saddam, Saddam
You are used to war games
Saddam, Saddam
We won't play this time
Saddam, Saddam
We can't leave you behind
Saddam, Saddam
This time we will get you
Saddam, Saddam
It is our virtue

You and Me

We are a lot alike
You and me
We are a lot alike
Let's just see

We need our health
To stay alive
We need bread and water
To survive

We love God
Me and you
God loves us
Yes he do

We want to be free
You and me
So we follow his law
The Deity

My Daddy

My daddy is gone
Far away
My daddy has left
He could not stay

My daddy went
To win a war
My daddy is gone
Oh so far

My daddy is strong
But he's not alone
It's a bad war
I hope he won't be long

My daddy is loved
We miss him a lot
And hope and pray
That he don't stay away

Come back daddy
We need you here
Come back daddy
We love you dear

Mommy

Mommy is a soldier
A soldier she is
Fast and smart
Just like a whiz

Mommy went away
To fight in a war
In another country
Oh so far

We love her so
And know things will get rough
She had to go
She is very tough

We try to spot
Her on TV
We miss her a lot
But it had to be

She'll be back soon
We pray to see
Her here again
With you and me

Why?

Does anyone know, why this had to be?
Does anyone know? It is hard to see

I only wonder
Why one would ponder
And use such thunder
But try not to blunder

To set a country free?

Does anyone know, why this had to be?
Does anyone know? It is hard to see

Now that they have arrived
And tearing up their lives
But what about their pride
And humanity and will
I guess they will
Just have to rebuild

Does anyone know, why this had to be?
Oh well, I guess I'll see, why it had to be!

Son

My son is at war
My son is so far
Away from home
But not alone
Other sons are there
Engaging in warfare

My son is strong
He has to be
To fight in a war
A war like the
War in Iraq
It's sad to see
What had to be
To free a people
From agony

My son is free
So he had to see
If he could help
Others be
I love my son
I need him so
I am so sad
He wanted to go

I hope and plea
To God above
To keep my son
Safe for me
I also plea
For the safety
Of all other sons
Fighting with he
To free Iraq
From misery

Baby

My daddy left before I was to arrive
With very long and dreadful good-byes
My dear daddy did not survive
He never saw me open my eyes

My daddy was killed in combat in Iraq
He was helping to set a country free
I really wish that I could have him back
I want him to be here with me

I love my daddy, he loves me too
I really miss him, mommy does too

He won't be here to help raise me
But I will make him proud
I know he misses me too
Daddy I will always love you

Daughter

My daughter
Went away to fight
In the war in Iraq
For me it's a plight

I didn't want her to go
I really miss and love her so
But she had to see
If she could help free
The many people
In misery

She's not alone
Other daughters are with her
It is hard to bear
The thought of her there
I wish she was here
She is oh so dear

I hope and pray
To God above
To keep them safe
They are really loved

Combatant

Army
Navy
Air Force
Marines

The Army is on the ground
The Navy is in the water around
The Air Force is up in the air
The Marines are everywhere

Our forces cover all of Iraq
Let's do what we came here to do
So that we won't have to come back

Our Dead

Those that perished
Will always be cherished

We will never forget them
And always remember when

They went to defend
Our country to the end

We love them so
We will never let them go

They were there for us
So it's OK to make a fuss

For something to remember them by
Here in the U.S., their country
For which they died

The British

The British are coming
The British are coming
Hail to the troops
The British are coming

The Brits are here
We are glad to see
To aid in the war
To set Iraq free

Their troops are strong
And very proud to be
They will stay their ground
They won't be knocked down

They were the only ones
That would do what was right
They stood with us on the ground
To release Iraq's people from their plight

Fear

Fear is deep
Within each of us
Fear is when
We do not trust

You should fear
If you are bad
You reap what you sow
If you are bad you must go

Saddam is bad
He should really fear
We are very mad
And getting near

We will get you yet
We are on our way
We will get you I bet
Hear what I say

Our Mighty Military

Our mighty military
They stand so tall
Our mighty military
Will not fall

Our mighty military
Stands united as one
Our mighty military
Your daughters and sons

Our might military
Is the strongest around
Our mighty military
Will never give up their ground

Our mighty military
Controls the air
Our mighty military
Has air power to spare

Our mighty military
Sails the oceans and seas
Our mighty military
Sails all waters with ease

Hero

A hero is one
That has courage you see
A hero is one
That will set you free

A hero is one
That you wold like to meet
A hero is one
That will not accept defeat

A hero is one
That will not hide
A hero is one
That will abide

A hero is one
That has a lot of pride
A hero is one
That has another hero
By his or her side

The Reporters Who Died

You were embedded
With the troops
You gave us the news
Right from the roots

We know it was rough
You were so tough
We are proud of you though
You didn't have to go

We are sad that you died
The troops still have to ride
For your and their pride
They will continue to strive

Effects

What will you be like
When you come back?
What will you be like
When you are not with the pack?

How will you cope
With what you've been through?
How will you cope
With the things that you viewed?

Will you be able to manage
Having the advantage
Of your family and country
Behind you?

We wish you well
Only time will tell
Come on home
We will avail

Wind

Sometimes it's a windy place
The wind blows hard against our face

It feels good if it is a very hot day
Hot, whoa, it is hard to say

We are fully clothed to be safe
From our boots to the mask on our face

But when we are not full of armor
The wind is nice if it is calm

Rain is good if it comes around
But it's so hot I doubt it hits the ground

Or maybe the wind blows it away
But that's OK we know the sand is going to stay

Sleep

Did somebody say sleep?
I don't remember how to sleep

I haven't had any in a week
Unless! I do it while I eat

I don't really know
If I sleep

Now is not the time
To get real deep

Into naps
Or other types of sleep

If you go to sleep
You may miss something if it's deep

Out here you never know
Who or what you will meet

So I just don't
Sleep
A lot!

The Coalition

The Coalition
Has a mission

They search for weapons
Of mass destruction

If they find any in their searches
They will find out where they were purchased

The weapons are very bad indeed
Those that know where they're hidden, need to cede

The knowledge so that the Coalition can find
And make sure not to leave any behind

When the Coalition finishes its work
Every country's worries will be released

And then we can all live in peace

The Cost of Freedom

The cost of freedom
Has risen in time.

Not only the money
And the lives on the line

But the souls and limbs
That are left behind

The cost of freedom
My God, what have we done?

Husbands, wives, mothers, fathers,
Daughters and sons

Hate continues to grow
Justice is always slow

We tend to lose faith
As we anticipate

Taskforce Ironhorse

Taskforce
Ironhorse

Oh oh

Nothing but POWER

They are the best
They've gotten their rest

Let them get started
They are ready to go
Let them get started
They are ready to blow

The bad out of Iraq
So that it never comes back

The power is here
More getting near

They are fired up
And ready to rumble

They will get it done
They are number one

BUFFALO SOLDIERS

My Poems

The way my poems sound
One would think I was there
Embedded with the troops
The ones on the ground

But I am not there
I'm safe here with you
Glued to my couch
And TV too

It is easy to feel
Sorrow for all
The video is real
I see how they fall

My poems are from my heart
The news gives them a start
I share them with you
So you can feel like you are there too

The People

The people are sad
You see
Why don't you just
Work with me
I'm here to help
And to restore your rights
But all that you seem to want to do is fight
Look at their faces
Falling to the ground
Their heartache and despair
From just looking around
Your family, your friends, your neighbors
You see
Why can't we both
Just let it be
Peace
For the people, you and me

Still Dying

We thought that it might be over
Yet here we are still dying
More and More
Each and everyday
Still dying

Sons and Daughters
Husbands and Wives
Fathers and Mothers
Sisters and Brothers
Still dying

The numbers keep rising
Adding two or more each day
Will it end?
Is all that we can say
And still hope
And still pray

Is It Over?

Not so loud
Not too scary
Not so loud
Much less wary

Maybe it'll end
Maybe it'll go away
Maybe the bombs will stop
And it'll be just another day

A quiet day
A silent array
A prayer in hand
In this Holy Land

Is it over yet?
How long can it last?
Is it over yet?
Allah please let it pass.